Morning
Java
—— with ——
Apostle Kimberly Armstrong

Morning Java

with

Apostle Kimberly Armstrong

Kimberly Armstrong

KASTRONG
MINISTRIES

MORNING JAVA WITH APOSTLE KIMBERLY
ARMSTRONG, Armstrong, Kimberly

1st ed.

KAstrong Ministries

KASTRONG
MINISTRIES

ISBN: 978-1-7340685-0-4

Table of Contents

Acknowledgements 9

A Note from Kimberly Armstrong 11

Chapter 1 *God Is Your Counselor* 15

Chapter 2 *Focus on What's Right* 23

Chapter 3 *The People Who Stayed* 31

Chapter 4 *God's Concealing Hand* 39

Chapter 5 *Your Impact on Others* 47

Chapter 6 *The Power of God's Word* 55

Chapter 7 *What You Believe You Can Achieve* 63

Chapter 8 *Staying Active in God* 71

Chapter 9 *Faith for the Impossible* 79

Chapter 10 *Seeing with God's Eyes* 87

Chapter 11 *You Are on the Way Up* 95

Chapter 12 *Moving into Tomorrow* 103

Chapter 13 *Only One You* 111

Chapter 14 *Stuck by Choice* 119

Chapter 15 *God Is Our Source*   125

Chapter 16 *Our Instructions*   131

Chapter 17 *A Relationship with God*   139

Chapter 18 *Letting Go of Just in Case*   145

Chapter 19 *Supporting God's Agenda*   151

About Kimberly Armstrong . . .   157

Acknowledgements:

I would like to take this time to thank God for gracing me, every morning with fresh Rhema to give to His people. He gave me the strength, the motivation and endurance to complete this assignment.

~~~

A special thank you to my family who supports and inspires me daily: my mother, Joyce Armstrong. My siblings: Rohn, Chad and Ashley. My nephews: Timothy and Emaj. All of your support and patience have proven to be invaluable. I am a reflection of you.

~~~

My spiritual mother/covering, Apostle Dr. Shirley R. Brown, for keeping me focused on what really matters most . . . ministry. I will forever be grateful for your prayers, support, time of pouring and labor of love.

~~~

My church family, MZCOD- The Healing Place, thank you for allowing me to be your Senior Leader during a time of spiritual transitioning, expansion and growth.

Special thank you to Terri Wooten-Parker and Chandra Williams. I am so grateful for your assistance and dedication. You both contributed in helping me keep my material on track and well organized. Your faithfulness was very well noted.

The Dunn family (Farley, Diane & Steven) your faith in me and the creativity that you have been graced with brought me to this place. Thank you for your support and your willingness to share your God-given gifts and resources.

I would like to thank all of those who were inspired by the daily quotes that I released on social media. It was your push for more that encouraged me to post something new and fresh every morning. Your personal testimonies motivated me to continue to inspire others.

A Note from Kimberly Armstrong

In all thy ways acknowledge the Lord and He will direct your path. This was one of the many scriptures that began to ring over and over in my spirit as I entered a time of testing. It all started in March of 2015. I had a series of things going on. They were ranging from my father fighting the good fight of faith in his battle against sickness to that of leading a church that was on the verge of transitioning into a much greater ministry. In the midst of that, my job as the director of two local community programs was on the precipice of change. God had something greater in mind far bigger than my finite mind could ever imagine.

When God is getting ready to take you to another dimension in Him, the flesh has to go through a process of elimination. Eliminating old emotions, hurts, disappointments, bitterness, anxieties, relationships, heartache as well as heartbreaks. All these and more have to be dealt with appropriately in order for healing and deliverance to take place in one's life. It was here that I was confronted with situations that would challenge my character. When you have been spoken evil of by the very ones that you spoke life into by the power of God, it will most definitely hurt the inward man. None of us are exempt from attacks. With so much happening around me I had to trust God to make sense of it all.

My assignment and purpose for being on the earth had reached a level in which my entire world was about to shift. This was a journey that no one could take for me. I had to travel alone. This process did not end overnight but lent itself to that of many, many nights. It was at the School of the Spirit in the Wilderness that I was able to hear His voice become stronger and walk in a deeper depth. None of this would have ever transpired if I had not submitted to God's will and way. On December 4, 2017, I was inspired to write a post on social media under the subject title, "God Has Granted Today."

God has granted today is a series of quotes that reassures you of God's grace and mercy extended towards you. Just knowing that

God has already made a way is comforting and gives you added strength to keep moving forward.

I never thought that from one post would come a series of posts. It was tiresome but God was using me to help someone get through their day. Yes, I wanted to stop. But then someone would message me and share their testimony of how they were being blessed. This compelled me to keep posting daily for an entire year.

Every morning, God gave me a fresh word to give to a new people. It is my prayer that these devotional quotes will encourage you as you face an unknown day with an all-knowing, ever-present, all-powerful God.

— Chapter 1 —

Have you considered . . .

Letting God be your Counselor vs. telling
your neighbor?

Scripture: Philippians 4:6-7 —

> *Do not be anxious about anything, but in every*
> *situation, by prayer and petition, with*
> *thanksgiving, present your requests to God.*
> *And the peace of God, which transcends all*
> *understanding, will guard your hearts and*
> *your minds in Christ Jesus.*

It is so amazing how we as a people will
seek out each other before we seek out God.
Typically, when the first unexpected thing

happens, we pick up the phone or go to social media and broadcast our personal matters to those that are really struggling with their own life issues. Have you heard the saying *misery loves company*? That is a true statement. When people are down, it makes them feel better to know that they are not the only ones. However, the best thing you can do is seek God concerning issues that only He knows about and only He can solve. People can lend an ear, but they cannot move God's hand. The change is only going to come when God moves on your behalf. Stop telling your neighbor and tell God.

God Has Granted Today:

Now take Full Possession of your Day!

Many times you may underestimate the power and the authority that have been released to you. However, once you recognize and believe in the One who gave the authority, you will take full possession of your day with no hesitation. God loves you and wants you to be assured that nothing can overtake what He overtook more than 2,000 years ago.

God Has Granted Today:

Walk in Authority and Not Intimidation!

God has created you in His image and in His likeness. He is your Father and He will not allow you to be overtaken by the wiles of the enemy. Trust in His Word and remember you were not given the spirit of fear but Power, Love and a Sound Mind.

God Has Granted Today:

Speak Life into what appears to be Dead Situations!

So many times you are defeated by the words that you speak. God never gave you a defeated tongue, but a tongue that will be used to move mountains to enact Kingdom Principles. This will cause you to be trium-phant in every aspect of life. So go ahead and Speak Life into what appears to be a dead situation.

— Chapter 2 —

Have you considered . . .

Most people focus more on what's not right vs. what is?

Scripture: Romans 7:19 —

> *For I do not do the good I want to do, but the evil I do not want to do—this I keep on doing.*

It is in the DNA of all humans to first react to things/situations that are not right. It just comes naturally because of the atmosphere into which we were born (called the world). This world gets rich off of wrong. Right tends to go unnoticed many times until something grand happens and draws attention to the situation. But most of the time it is negative actions that get the biggest coverage. But you can make a conscious decision to praise right and avoid conversations concerning wrong. This way, what's not right will not get as much momentum as it should.

God Has Granted Today:

Be thankful for being a part of the Portrait!

So many things can happen to you during the night and throughout the course of a day. However, God has angels that are charged over you. They will continue to serve you until He says well done. Until then, be glad today is not that day. He included you in the family portrait. Smile, for He is smiling with you.

God Has Granted Today:

Trust Him with the rest of Yours!

You may have been hurt, disappointed and perhaps betrayed by people that you thought would be there for you. Only to find out at the end of the day they were not This doesn't mean that you can place God on their level. He is nothing like man. He's the creator of man and the Father of the Son. Trust Him with all of your day. He is your assurance that everything will work out in your favor.

God Has Granted Today:

Find the Good in Everything . . .
No matter what!

I know that sometimes it is hard to find good in things that may appear to be so bad. However, in everything you can find something good. Look a little closer, search a little harder, and in the midst of the rubble you will find at least one gem. Hold on to it.

— *Chapter 3* —

Have you considered . . .

Taking time to thank God for the people who stayed with you vs. talking about those who left you?

Scripture: Acts 28:15 —

> *The brothers and sisters there had heard that we were coming, and they traveled as far as the Forum of Appius and the Three Taverns to meet us. At the sight of these people Paul thanked God and was encouraged.*

Don't overlook those that stayed with you in the hardest of days and/or times. It is these that you can say are true friends or have been assigned to you. However, it doesn't matter how many are with you. If the one that you thought would always be there isn't, it brings about a hurt that is indescribable. But at the end of the day, just realize that God revealed to you who and what was real and/or fake. After you get over the hurt and letdowns, you will see that it was the best thing that could have ever happened.

God Has Granted Today:

Don't waste time on Lost Time . . . Make New!

Let go of what you could not do or a bad choice that you may have made. That part of your life is over and has expired. The moments might be gone, but the lessons you learned during that time will last a lifetime. Learn from them and seek God for clear concise directions, so that you can prevent the past from repeating itself. It is time for the NEW to begin with YOU.

God Has Granted Today:

Start Fresh . . . Walk in the New and Live in Your Now!

Rise up and do as the Apostle Paul did when the viper bit him. He shook if off. Others watched in amazement, waiting to see him become deathly ill, but needless to say, it did not happen. He maintained his faith and confidence in God. As a result, he was able to move past the expectation of others and walk in the miraculous presence of the almighty God.

God Has Granted Today:

Celebrate your Winnings!

It's a joyful day full of praises to our Lord and Savior Jesus Christ. It is He that has made you win. This win will continue throughout your lifetime. Many were hoping that you would stay in your losing season. Needless to say, that was not what God had planned. You have so much to be thankful for in your winning season. So take some time and do inventory. Celebrate your winnings! After all, it is your celebration!

— Chapter 4 —

Have you considered . . .

That God will sometimes conceal a thing so that you will not get caught up in foolishness!

Scripture: Proverbs 25:2 —

> *It is the glory of God to conceal a matter; to search out a matter is the glory of kings.*

God is omniscient. He knows everything from the beginning to the end. As a result, He will keep you from seeing an opportunity or having involvement with people that will cause you to end up in a heap of trouble. As you continue to seek the right answer, you will find it. God's love for you is immeasurable. He will do whatever it takes to keep you focused on your earthly assignment.

God Has Granted Today:

Don't look through the Shades of Negativity but through the Lenses of Positivity!

It is easy to find negativity in anything. Negativity is a tool that the enemy uses to keep you from striving for more. However, if you keep a positive outlook, when faced with life's challenges, your outcome will be different. Do not see your challenges for what they are but for the purpose in why they were sent. Remember, the enemy would like for you to fulfill his destiny for your life. So it is of grave importance that you are focused and see out of the lenses that God has prescribed. You will immediately begin to see victory open doors and new opportunities.

God Has Granted Today:

He Discharged you from Yesterday's Uncertainties . . . Today He affords you all His Promises!

Not letting go of your past mistakes and reminiscing over poor choices that you made can keep you in a place of stagnation. God did not intend for you to be stuck in your past. He has freed you from that bondage so that you can freely receive His promises. The future is so bright. He has filled it with every good thing. Receive His labor of love.

God Has Granted Today:

Fear Wasn't Invited! But Power, Love and a Sound Mind Were!

Don't let intimidation, anxiety and fear keep you from operating in your God-given purpose. You were designed to walk in Love, demonstrate Power and operate with a Sound Mind! Do not become paralyzed by Fear but come alive and move into that place that has your name on it. Remember, Fear wasn't invited but Power, Love and a Sound Mind are waiting for you to ask them to be your dance partner.

— Chapter 5 —

Have you considered . . .

Your role in any situation, whether Positive or Negative, will have a strong impact on the outcome!!

Scripture: Proverbs 17:22 —

> *A cheerful heart is good medicine, but a crushed spirit dries up the bones.*

Examine yourself and be mindful of how you respond to any given situation. Your reaction will have a major effect on whether or not the outcome will be favorable. If you are joyful in spirit you will have a healthier outcome. But anger or negative vibes may cause your outcome to end badly. Remember, many will be recipients of the decisions you make. So think beyond yourself and make choices that will benefit others greatly. Your decisions just may be the key to how everything will end.

God Has Granted Today:

Greet Him properly! For He is the Answer you seek!

Give honor to whom honor is due. Even in the model prayer, you are admonished to give Him honor and the respect due His name. For example, *Our Father which Art in Heaven, Hallowed Be Thy Name.* It is He that provides all good things to you. Never allow yourself to speak to Him or about Him in a derogatory way. He's the heartbeat, your life's existence and pulse of your answered prayer.

God Has Granted Today:

Be that Glimmer of Hope that others need to see!

Darkness looms at every turn and seeks to cause you to stumble. However, because you have the true light abiding within you, it yields brightness that gives others hope. That glimmer can be someone's Beacon of Light.

God Has Granted Today:

Walk in the Authority that Jesus's Blood paid for!

Purchase with Authority and Boldness everything that Jesus' Blood paid for. Don't live in confusion when God gave you freedom from fear. Don't live in the land of "I can't" when Jesus' blood says you can. His blood can purchase what natural currency and coins cannot.

— *Chapter 6* —

Have you considered . . .

The more of God's Word you know and live, the bigger threat you are to the adversary!!

Scripture: 2 Timothy 2:15 —

> *Do your best to present yourself to God as one approved, a worker who does not need to be ashamed and who correctly handles the word of truth.*

Get loaded up with all the Word that you can. This is your ammunition against the workings of the enemy. He knows the Word, but he doesn't like for the Word to be used against him. Be purposeful in your studying and pray and ask God to give you deliberate strategies that you can use against the dream killer. Live the Word that you read and make the adversary wish he had never come your way!

God Has Granted Today:

Choose to be Love in Action . . . not Love Unnoticed!

Many face uncertainties throughout the day as well as at night. So much so, they never notice the love that is shown towards them. Today, demonstrate love intentionally. Make it a point to let someone know that love came to check in with them. Go the extra mile.

God Has Granted Today:

Stay Focused on all things that Matter . . . Let Everything Else fade into the Background!

Don't let the fringes of life take your mind off of the entire outfit and/or garment of life. Many things will attempt to challenge your faith and try to distract you from what really matters. Let those things fade like a fall leaf that loses its color and soon returns back to the earth.

God Has Granted Today:

Don't let Past Appointments cause you to miss your Next Appointment!

Do you remember those friends called Should Have, Could Have and Would Have? These were the past appointments that you missed. Don't hold on so strongly to the missed opportunities that you are unable to hear the knock of change that's coming to bring you your next appointment.

— *Chapter 7* —

Have you considered . . .

Just believing and achieving!!

Scripture: Mark 11:24 —

Therefore I tell you, whatever you ask for in prayer, believe that you have received it, and it will be yours.

Believing can be hard. Sometimes it seems as if it is easier to believe for someone else's breakthroughs than it is when you are facing your own crisis. That's a trick of the enemy. Use your voice and make your personal request known to your heavenly Father. Do not allow your blessings to be withheld from you especially when all you have to do is reach out to God for help. He does not respect one person over another. He did it for others, and He will surely do it for you. Just believe and then you will achieve.

God Has Granted Today:

Be the Difference that others will feel Compelled to Follow!

There are many false doctrines being taught by false leaders. They are leading many, but the end results of their teachings are deadly. God needs you to be that one that will lead by example where they can see manifested results. It will cause those you lead to change directions and follow a path that will produce life. A life that's not filled with deception and/or false hope. You were chosen to be the difference.

God Has Granted Today:

Receive the Plans He has for your Life!

Stop looking at what others are doing. Be thankful that God has specific plans for your life. Go forth and be the best "you" that you can be on this side of Glory. You are packed full of purpose and plans. Receive and Release!

God Has Granted Today:

Take a moment to say Thank You!

A thank you from a sincere heart makes room for more blessings. Take time to tell God thank you for the many doors He has opened and even the ones He has closed. It just takes a moment. Surely you have time to thank the King of Kings and the Lord of Lords.

— *Chapter 8* —

Have you considered . . .

Inactivity in the things of God will cause stagnation within the House of God!!

Scripture: Ecclesiastes 10:18 —

> *Through laziness, the rafters sag; because of idle hands, the house leaks.*

Do not stop doing the things of God. Whatever He has placed in your hands to do, keep doing it. Once you stop, it will be hard to get back in that place that you once were. Your spirit man has to be strengthened and fed by the spiritual matters of God. When you neglect feeding your spirit, you open yourself up to selfish desires. Eventually these desires will start dictating what they crave and will and will not do. This will affect the house of God tremendously.

God Has Granted Today:

It was worth the Push!

Going through a process of giving birth to spiritual blessings can be costly. It will cost you everything and nothing can be a stand in. But the joy of the morning is worth the push. The windows of Heaven will open and Victory will become your new brand.

God Has Granted Today:

The Birth of Our Champion: He was born to Declare Us Winners! We win because He was born!

Because your spiritual DNA is from your Heavenly Father, he creates and makes nothing but champions. It runs through your spiritual veins. You have won every battle that you have ever faced. God made you that way. You are made a champion, because your Father is the Champion of Champions.

God Has Granted Today:

Negativity is contagious!

Why? Because, we were born in a sinful world where negativity is bred. However, if you are a born-again believer with a renewed mind you will not allow negative situations to make you a negative person. Optimism will bring positive results. Whereas negativity will always bring unwelcomed events into your life. Don't give negativity permission to become a fixture in your life.

— *Chapter 9* —

Have you considered . . .

The very thing that looks impossible is actually depending on your Faith for its possibility!!

Scripture: Matthew 17:20 —

> *He replied, "Because you have so little faith.*
> *Truly I tell you, if you have faith as small as a*
> *mustard seed, you can say to this mountain,*
> *'Move from here to there,' and it will move.*
> *Nothing will be impossible for you."*

Don't settle for what you think can't be done. Why? Because all things are possible with God. However, your faith must at least be the size of a grain of a mustard seed. What looks hopeless is only waiting to connect with your faith. It is at that point that you will soon see the power of possibility. God has the power to reverse or remove whatever the enemy tried to keep from coming forth.

God Has Granted Today:

Even when silence is loud . . . it is in the Quietness of Praise that Breakthrough springs forth!

When you are faced with uncertainty and you can't seem to hear God speak, drown out the silence with your praise. When you are seeking direction and the sound of nothing becomes too loud, drown out the silence with praise. It is in this decision that you will find purpose and spiritual guidance. Do not become discouraged along the way, but praise your way through the traffic of your thoughts. Again, I say drown out the noise of the silence with your praise and watch *Breakthrough* spring forth.

God Has Granted Today:

Provision has been provided! Journey onward!

Be reminded of the writings of the Apostle Paul. He testified that in times of need, his God would supply all of them according to His riches in Glory through Christ Jesus. Everything that you need has been provided for you. Continue your journey and know that your journey has been carefully mapped out and well thought through by God Himself.

God Has Granted Today:

Remember your need is never Greater than His Hand! He's got you!

God has everything, and everything belongs to Him. The needs that you may have do not compare to the resources that He has made available for you. What He has is more than what you need. He reminds us that He owns a thousand hills with cattle on them. Can you imagine what that would look like? This is beyond your attempt to imagine. He is the God of More Than Enough.

— *Chapter 10* —

Have you considered . . .

Your perception of your problem is magnified but God's Perception of it is already done!!

Scripture: Ephesians 1:3 —

> *Praise be to the God and Father of our Lord Jesus Christ, who has blessed us in the heavenly realms with every spiritual blessing in Christ.*

You may tend to waiver when facing a problem. At times you may look at the problem, and it looks so scary, causing you to fear the worst. However, you must settle your spirit and realize that God knew about the problem way before you did. He works from an It Is Finished point of view. Where He sits, it is already finished. This should create a sense of peace in knowing that He has already done or solved what you were so gravely concerned about. He's God and no one can compete with Him. Your problem is really your processing.

God Has Granted Today:

Remember He travels with you everywhere you go! You are never alone. Acknowledge Him!

He never allows you to move without having you covered by His presence. He has assigned you your own personal set of Angels. They will serve, maintain and sustain you while you are on duty here on earth. You are never alone.

God Has Granted Today:

Take note of the little things . . . they pave the way to Bigger and Better Things! He is your Way Maker!

Take some time to intentionally acknowledge that blessings are all around you. The little things are important to take note of because they will lead to bigger and better things. It is mentioned in scripture that we are not to despise small beginnings. We are to be good stewards over what we have been given. Then He will give us more. Stay alert and appreciative and watch what the Way Maker will do on your behalf.

God Has Granted Today:

Be Thankful that you were chosen for Greatness . . . Accept Nothing Less!

There are those you may affiliate with on a daily basis that may not understand or have been taught that they have purpose. Without that knowledge you will never know the fullness of your potential. But God spelled it out for us, and He said, "I have chosen you; you did not choose me." He also reminded us that many are called but few are chosen. The chosen will stand out because of the greatness within them.

— *Chapter 11* —

Have you considered . . .

That your lowest point is only an indicator of just how high God is going to take you . . . Praise Him!!

Scripture: Mark 10:29-30 —

> *"Truly I tell you," Jesus replied, "no one who has left home or brothers or sisters or mother or father or children or fields for me and the gospel will fail to receive a hundred times as much in this present age: homes, brothers, sisters, mothers, children and fields—along with persecutions—and in the age to come eternal life."*

The testing that you are currently facing is a strong indicator of how God is going to bless you. God is one that will cut back in one area in order to gain more in another area. This process is not a fun day or a walk in the park. However, just hold on and realize God is going to bless you double for every trouble that you have encountered. Nothing is done in vain. It will be rewarded, so hold on and keep the faith.

God Has Granted Today:

For Direction . . . Listen to that still small voice . . . Tune out the most obvious!

Many times what seems to be the most obvious, turns out to be the wrong path to follow. If you would listen to that still small voice that is giving you direction, most of the time you will arrive on time and at the right place. It is so important that you stay tuned in to that still small voice.

God Has Granted Today:

Stay focused on the bigger picture! Dream Big!

Do not be distracted but stay focused on your end game. That is to say, Dream Big so that your future will be greater than your now. This can happen only if you stay focused and do what is required of you. Follow the instructions and be led by the Holy Spirit. He will enable you to see your dream become a reality. Dream Big!

God Has Granted Today:

Don't let this last set of 24 hours Trip you up and cause you to Miss your Next!

No time for Foolery. There is too much at stake. When you focus on your last 24 hours, you lose sight of the bigger picture. The weight of yesterday is a detriment to where you are heading. Stop tripping over words that were spoken to you over things that were insignificant. Step over them and move into your Next.

— *Chapter 12* —

Have you considered . . .

That what you are going through will soon be what you went through!

Scripture: James 1:2-4 —

> *Consider it pure joy, my brothers and sisters, whenever you face trials of many kinds, because you know that the testing of your faith produces perseverance. Let perseverance finish its work so that you may be mature and complete, not lacking anything.*

All of the problems that you face will soon be a testament of your faith. You will no longer refer to your problems in the present tense. They will be placed in the archives of your past. You will look back and see how God brought you to a victorious place. So celebrate now what soon will be your Next.

God Has Granted Today:

The devil tried to keep you in yesterday . . . but God gave you a Brand-New Day!

The enemy is powerless but would like for you to think otherwise. He will attempt to do many things, but unless he has been granted permission by God, he cannot carry out any of his plans.

God overrode the enemy's decision to bring death to you during the night, in the early morning hours and/or during the day. It is good to know that you have a Heavenly Father that seeks no harm to you but is always looking out for your betterment.

God gives you a brand-new start every morning. He does not operate in yesterday's residue. So move forward knowing that the way has been paved and ways have been made for you to get the most out of this day.

God Has Granted Today:

Do not return to the same routine of old. Try a new route . . . get better results!

It is natural for you to return to a routine that seemed natural for you at some point in time. However, you are in a new season now, and what worked before will not work now. Do not be afraid to step out and try something new. You will get better results. Confuse the enemy and make him remember that he is not in control of your destiny.

God Has Granted Today:

Choose to be an extension of His Grace towards others in need of Mercy! He freely gave to us, so we freely give!

Never forget where you came from and who God used to help you. Pay it forward. Be that hand that reaches to lift someone up. Be willing to forgive others that have erred along the way. Show them the love of Jesus and grant them opportunities that they never would have received from those that are not in right relationship with the Father. Remember, it was God's grace that helped you escape what should have killed you. So follow His example and give to those that are in need of a second chance and so on. Give as you have been given.

— Chapter 13 —

Have you considered . . .

Loving the fact that you are the only you that
there will ever be . . . Be impactful!

Scripture: Psalms 139:14 —

*I praise you because I am fearfully and
wonderfully made; your works are wonderful, I
know that full well.*

Be comfortable in the skin that you're in.
There is only one of you and there will never
be another. Make a lasting impression on
others, so that well after your footprints are
no longer available on this side of life, others
will still be captivated by what you accom-

plished on the earth.

God Has Granted Today:

Do not be Afraid. Speak . . . He will Hear and Respond!

Talk to the one that really understands what you are facing and the direction in which you are headed. Let God lead you in the way in which you should go. No one knows the plan for your life but Him. So, go ahead and talk to Him about what's concerning you. Don't hold anything back. He will not judge you but only love you. Give Him the opportunity to prove that He has heard you and has the power to deliver.

God Has Granted Today:

Take time to realize just how Blessed you are! The Greater One is on your side!

Every now and then you need to take time to see just how blessed you are. How you once were confused but now you have direction. You were in lack, but God provided everything you stood in need of. So when faced with dreary circumstances, just remember how God moved for you in times past and He will move again now. Give Him the opportunity to show you where you came from and where He is taking you. He is 100% team YOU.

God Has Granted Today:

Make every effort to enjoy it! Don't be cheated by worrying. It cannot change what God has given!

Be grateful and confident that God had you in mind on this day. So make every moment count. Do not get caught up in overthinking a situation. It will lead to worrying if you are not careful. Worrying is the inability to see resolve with any given situation. It cannot add or take from what God has ordained for your life. Rest in knowing that He is smarter, wiser, kinder and all powerful. God's promises are true and sure. Therefore, if you can bring your flesh under subjection and let the Spirit show you the way, then your days will be filled with much joy. Do not allow unseen results to cause you to miss this day that God has prepared with you in mind. Enjoy, my friend, enjoy!

— *Chapter 14* —

Have you considered . . .

That you and/or others may be stuck by choice and not by design . . . checkout the true motives!

Scripture: Joshua 24:15 —

> *But if serving the Lord seems undesirable to you, then choose for yourselves this day whom you will serve, whether the gods your ancestors served beyond the Euphrates, or the gods of the Amorites, in whose land you are living. But as for me and my household, we will serve the Lord.*

Deliverance is available for all who will

receive it. Some people prefer to remain ill and stuck in unpleasant situations because that has become their norm. Sadly to say it has also become their happy place. They use their condition as an excuse not to move forward. But this is not how it should be. You have been given power over all unclean things. God has also given us His Son's Name to use in order to speak to everything that is causing us uneasiness. Don't get stuck in this rut but start examining your motives to determine why you are in the state that you are in. Make another choice that will bring life to you and/or others.

God Has Granted Today:

Regardless of how things look . . . Just know He will get the Glory! He specializes in making you look Good!

Do not let your mind be overshadowed by the hopelessness that you may be sensing. It is only a feeling which is an emotion. Your feelings are not factual but just substantial. But trust this, God loves you and He will do whatever it takes to make you succeed. There's no need to worry and no need to fear. Your situation has been orchestrated so that others will recognize that He is God and God alone. He specializes in making you look better than you should.

God Has Granted Today:

Take time to Laugh! It's good for the Soul!

Find a good movie or spend some time with friends and laugh. Many are afraid of too much laughter. They feel as if sorrow or trouble is just around the corner. These are the ones that are serious about and over-thinking everything. Nevertheless, you will find that if you take time to laugh it will strengthen you. It will cause you to look at key issues, circumstances and other troubling factors through different eyes. Let laughter relieve you of unwanted stress. Your soul will be better for it.

— *Chapter 15* —

Have you considered . . .

Acknowledging that God is the Source behind all of your success and not you?

Scripture: 2 Corinthians 3:5 —

> *Not that we are competent in ourselves to claim anything for ourselves, but our competence comes from God.*

Always remember that it is God that has called you and not you yourself. All of your success has been God-given. He is the source of all and every good thing that has happened to you. Give Him all the glory for all the wonderful things that he has done and will continue to do.

God Has Granted Today:

Dare to Dream! Expect the Dream-giver to bring it to pass!

Remember we are spirit beings serving an Almighty God. Purpose has been breathed into you and the path has been made clear. Do not allow what you see and/or life's circumstances to cause you to miss out on the great opportunity that has been mapped out for you. Your end will be great. Go forth with greatness in mind. Remember that no one can do what God has placed within you to do. Expect nothing less than God's best for your life. Make the devil regret the day that you dared to dream.

God Has Granted Today:

Walk by Faith and not by 20/20. 20/20 will never secure the promise!

When you look at life through the lens of self, you always come up with the wrong portrait. The colors will be off and the focus will not be clear. However, when you see life through the eyes of Jesus, everything is perfectly positioned and picture frame ready. Your own vision will never secure the promise. Only by Faith can you be sure of an on-time delivery.

— *Chapter 16* —

Have you considered . . .

Following through with the last set of instructions you received? Obedience will get you the results you seek!

Scripture: Luke 11:28 —

> *Blessed rather are those who hear the word of God and obey it.*

You have sought for answers to your situation and God has answered your prayers. Not just one time but time and time again. Now you are asking Him for more instructions. Go ahead and follow what he has already told you to do and everything will be alright. If not, you are only delaying your time of true happiness.

God Has Granted Today:

Faith It 'til you MAKE IT!

There are times when believing seems so hard to do. Especially after a wait that seems as if it will never end. So don't allow what it looks like to you and your counterparts to cause you to Fake your End Results. This type of behavior never ends well. Be encouraged, because God is overflowing with promises and He always delivers. So never give up. Keep feeding your faith with the Word of the Living God. Keep pushing until you see the Results that faking could never bring to the table. Your faith in God is what's going to catapult you into your Next.

God Has Granted Today:

Just know that you are closer today than you were yesterday to that Open Door!

Get ready, get ready, get ready! Today, you have arrived in a place that brings you closer to that Open Door that you have been anxiously awaiting. You are closer now than you were three weeks ago, three days or even 3 minutes ago. Begin to praise God for giving you the strength to move into another day, another moment with purpose in your heart.

God Has Granted Today:

Prepare to secure your open door! Do your part so He can do HIS!

You must be ready for what's behind the open door. You can't wait until the door is open to start getting ready. Start making preparation for your promise even while your flesh is making you feel as if it will not happen. Just know when this happens, it is a strong indicator that God is going to make it happen for you. Listen closely to what the Spirit says to you and follow the instructions given. Remember, you must do your part in the natural as God gives you orders from the Spirit.

— Chapter 17 —

Have you considered?

Building a relationship with God versus having religious moments!!

Scripture: Matthew 6:5; 22:37 —

> *Jesus replied: "'Love the Lord your God with all your heart and with all your soul and with all your mind.' And when you pray, do not be like the hypocrites, for they love to pray standing in the synagogues and on the street corners to be seen by others. Truly I tell you, they have received their reward in full."*

Religion is only as good as the moments that you are ritually engaged in or practicing it. Note the word practicing. It becomes dutiful, routine and mundane. However, relationship is built on something that is much more meaningful. You become one with Him in sharing your most intimate thoughts and desires. You cherish every moment that you spend in His presence. Relationship develops into your lifestyle and creates a natural love for God.

God Has Granted Today:

Walk in Truth, Be His Reflection and make Him Proud!

This seems like it is so hard, and you are so right. For our flesh will always try to drown out the voice of the Spirit. It is and has always been a battle. However, you have been given the power to overcome and prove to the defeated one that you are a Son and/or Female Son of the Most High God. Walk in the truth of the word of God and be a reflection of God's love. In doing this you will make Him proud to be your Heavenly Father.

God Has Granted Today:

Be not afraid to share your heart with Him!

Do you sometimes feel that no one understands or can relate to what you are going through? Of course you do! But never be afraid to tell God all about it. He loves it when you talk with Him about what's on your heart. There is nothing that you are thinking or facing that He doesn't already know. You do know that He is omniscient or all-knowing. So let transparency be the order of the day. By the way, you may be surprised how the conversation ends.

— Chapter 18 —

Have you considered . . .

Letting go of your just-in-case thinking and just trust God with your case!

Scripture: Matthew 6:25 —

> *Therefore I tell you, do not worry about your life, what you will eat or drink; or about your body, what you will wear. Is not life more than food, and the body more than clothes?*

Yes, you may have been told by friends and/or relatives that you need to put aside a little something just in case you have a rainy day. Well, there's nothing wrong with that as long as the instructions came from God. If not, then you are trusting in what you can do for yourself and not what God can do for you as your Father. Learn to rest in Him and let Him lead, guide and provide for you. Trust Him because He knows what's best for you!

God Has Granted Today:

Go Forth and Believe He heard you!

Wow! It is so fascinating how when you finally released that prayer, that heaven released your answer. Now from this day forward expect the delivery of the promise to come. God heard you and gave your angels the go ahead to make it all come to pass. There is a praise somewhere deep within you that is patiently waiting to come out. Go ahead and make the defeated one angry and give God a 30-second praise. He Heard YOU!

God Has Granted Today:

Lift your hands, raise your voice and rejoice for Jesus Christ is Lord!

Start your day off with a mighty shout of triumph. For the day may be filled with set ups from the defeated one, but your shout will announce to him that your God is greater. Go ahead and set the tone for your day and let God clear your path. He is Lord!!!!

— *Chapter 19* —

Have you considered . . .

Being supportive to God's Kingdom Agenda by being an Active Participant!

Scripture: Romans 12:5 —

> *So in Christ we, though many, form one body,*
> *and each member belongs to all the others.*

The Body of Christ is in need of all of your spiritual giftings. We need you to stand with us, be active and help push God's Kingdom Agenda. The war against the kingdom of darkness is intensifying and we need all hands on deck. He has invested so much good in you. Stand your ground and do not get caught up with the ways of the world.

God Has Granted Today:

Do not be Reactionary . . . Just Respond Appropriately!

Be wise and think smart. Do not allow your deep-rooted desires to cause you to do something that will jeopardize what you have long waited for. You have prayed, praised and worshiped too long to allow one moment of emotional release to cause you to lose everything. Be alert in the spirit and recognize the defeated one when he's at work. Respond the way a true son would. You've got this! Let the Father deal with all that other stuff. Be wise and think smart.

God Has Granted Today:

Even when times seem uncertain, put your Trust in the One who is Certain!

You've been here before. Did not God come through for you then? Yes, and He is going to come through for you this time. Take a moment, check His record and see that He has a 100% success record by all who put their trust in Him. There is no change in Him. He is always certain and sure.

About Kimberly Armstrong . . .

Apostle Kimberly Armstrong, is the daughter of Mrs. Joyce Armstrong and the late Mr. William H. Armstrong of Mount Olive, North Carolina. She currently resides in Goldsboro, North Carolina. Apostle Armstrong is a powerful woman of God who with grace, commitment, and passion serves as Senior Pastor of Mount Zion Church of Deliverance- The Healing Place in Calypso, North Carolina. She is also the Founder of KASTRONG Ministries, Goldsboro, North Carolina, a ministry of empowerment that is designed to reach the broken in spirit. She has been called for "such a time as this" to bring a message of deliverance to the shackled in spirit and healing to the broken with a cutting-edge delivery that changes all who come into her presence.

The Word she brings forth is founded in the bedrock of Scripture and ignited by the Holy Spirit to enrich, challenge and inspire the hearts and souls of God's people. Apostle Armstrong ministers the unadulterated Word of God with such a revelatory yet practical teaching gift, it reaches all hearers directly at their point of need and ushers them into a place of eternal freedom. She ministers with authority and clarity. Her objective is to deliver the uncompromising Word of God so that people will be propelled into living the Word and applying it to their everyday walk. She will encourage, equip and empower every hearer with the written and spoken Word. Her warm heart and giving spirit are immeasurable.

For many years, she has worked diligently with the youth throughout the state of North Carolina. She has held many professional positions ranging from President of Majestic Shalom Ministries Inc.; Founder and Executive Director of The Connect Four Family Program, Goldsboro, North Carolina; Director of the Upward Bound Program at Fayetteville State University; to that of working as an Administrator within the Wayne County Public School System. Her educational background ranges from an Associate Degree in Developmental Disabilities, a Bachelor's Degree in Psychology, to that of a Master's Degree in Administration. She wants you to know that the most important aspect in her life is her relationship with God and being an ambassador for the Kingdom of God. She is tearing down satanic strongholds and helping others get their breakthrough in God. This is worth more than words can ever express. God is doing great things through this consecrated vessel.

www.ingramcontent.com/pod-product-compliance
Lightning Source LLC
Chambersburg PA
CBHW051840090426
42736CB00011B/1897